ALTERNATOR BOOKS™

PICTURES to PARAGRAPHS

WRITING A REPORT

Heather E. Schwartz

Lerner Publications ◆ Minneapolis

Lerner Publications Company
An imprint of Lerner Publishing Group, Inc.
241 First Avenue North
Minneapolis, MN 55401 USA

For reading levels and more information, look up this title at www.lernerbooks.com.

Main body text set in Aptifer Sans LT Pro.
Typeface provided by Linotype AG.

Editor: Nicole Berglund **Designer:** Emily Harris **Photo Editor:** Angel Kidd

Library of Congress Cataloging-in-Publication Data

Names: Schwartz, Heather E. author
Title: Writing a report / Heather E. Schwartz.
Description: Minneapolis : Lerner Publications, 2026. | Series: Pictures to paragraphs | Includes bibliographical references and index. | Audience: Ages 8–12 | Audience: Grades 4–6 | Summary: "We use reports to share researched information at school or at work. Students learn how to write a report through examples and writing prompts based on photos"— Provided by publisher.
Identifiers: LCCN 2025016368 (print) | LCCN 2025016369 (ebook) | ISBN 9798765688793 library binding | ISBN 9798348028787 paperback | ISBN 9798765695906 epub
Subjects: LCSH: Report writing—Juvenile literature
Classification: LCC LB1047.3 .S39 2026 (print) | LCC LB1047.3 (ebook) | DDC 371.30281—dc23/eng/20250501

LC record available at https://lccn.loc.gov/2025016368
LC ebook record available at https://lccn.loc.gov/2025016369

Manufactured in the United States of America
1-1012674-54709-6/25/2025

TABLE OF CONTENTS

Sharing the Facts 4

CHAPTER 1
GETTING STARTED 6

CHAPTER 2
DEVELOPING YOUR TOPIC 12

CHAPTER 3
DELIVERING YOUR INFORMATION 20

CHAPTER 4
PUTTING IT ALL TOGETHER................26

Glossary 30
Learn More 31
Index 32

SHARING THE FACTS

Joe loved studying languages. When his teacher assigned a report and said students could choose their own topics, Joe knew this was his chance to share his knowledge! When you're interested in a topic, learning about it can be fun. Once you have a collection of fascinating facts, you can share them in a report.

The first step to writing a report is creating an outline. An outline helps writers organize their thoughts into a writing plan. After the outline, they write a draft. They share this draft with others for feedback. Writers use feedback to evaluate what needs work. Then they revise the draft to make their report stronger.

At the last stage of writing, writers edit to correct spelling and grammar errors. A strong, polished report might be good enough to publish! Students often write reports as school assignments. But reports can be useful outside of school too. They are an opportunity to teach people about a topic that matters to you. Your report could inspire them to learn even more.

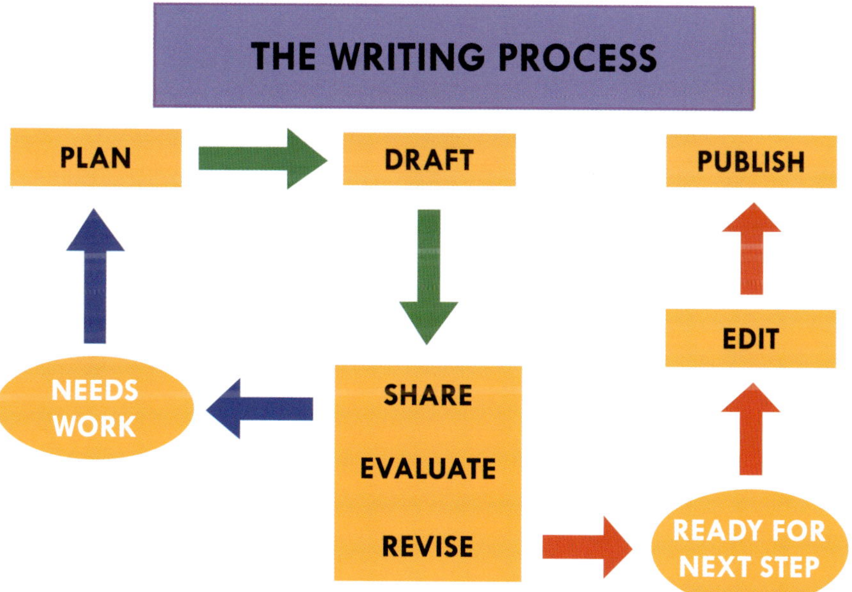

CHAPTER 1
GETTING STARTED

What will you write your report about? Sometimes you can pick anything you like. Other times, your teacher might assign you to write about science, a book you've read, or a specific time in history. In any case, aim to choose a topic that makes you feel excited to research and write. That excitement will show in your work from the outline stage to the final version.

Think of your outline as a plan for your draft. It includes three parts: an introduction, a body, and a conclusion. The body will include three to five paragraphs of information. This is the heart of your report. When you're creating your outline, take note of the details that are most exciting and unusual about your topic. This is great material to include in your introduction and expand on in your body paragraphs.

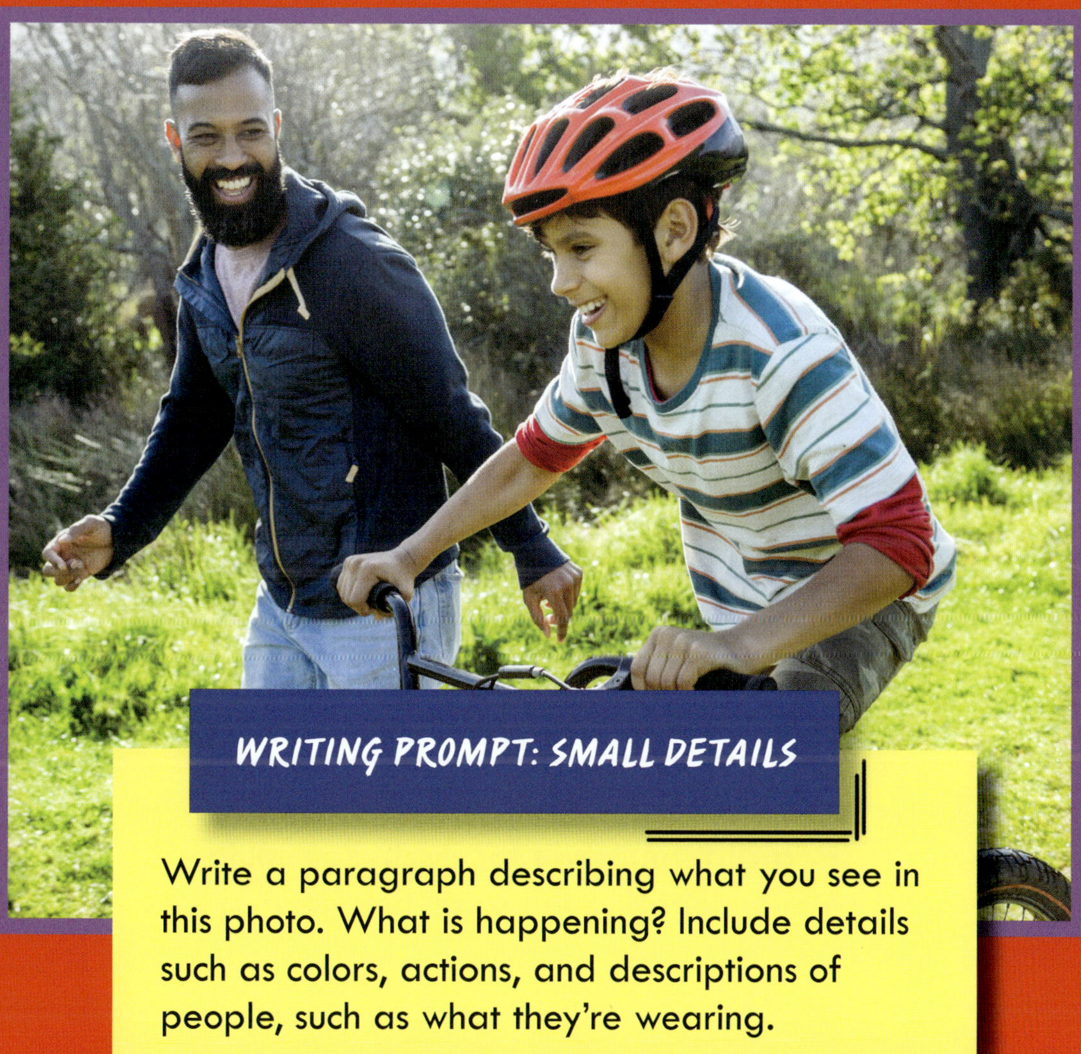

WRITING PROMPT: SMALL DETAILS

Write a paragraph describing what you see in this photo. What is happening? Include details such as colors, actions, and descriptions of people, such as what they're wearing.

Even before readers get to the introduction, they'll read something else first—the title! Some writers like to brainstorm ideas for titles after writing their introduction or even after writing their first draft. Others prefer to start with title ideas that can help them focus their outline.

Titles are often short, clever, and creative. The best titles are catchy—as in they catch readers' attention. At the same time, your title needs to be honest. It needs to represent what's really in the report, not just attract attention. A title that's overly dramatic might even repel readers. They may be excited by the headline only to be disappointed by the content.

WRITING PROMPT: TACKLING TITLES

Write three possible titles inspired by this photo. Try a different style for each. You could use alliteration, or using the same first letter in every word. You could try rhyming, humor, one word, or multiple words.

The introduction is the first part of your report. It prepares readers for what they're about to read and lets them know what topic you're covering. A good introduction draws readers in and invites them to continue reading.

Consider how you might go one step further in your introduction. You could draw attention by asking questions that need answers. Or you could mention unusual facts that need more explanation. This could inspire readers to guess at the answers. They will keep reading because they expect to learn more in your body paragraphs. And it's your job to make sure they do!

WRITING PROMPT: BUILDING SUSPENSE

Look at this image and imagine what might happen next. Will the ball go through the basket? Will a player get knocked to the ground? How will the players react? How will the crowd react? Write an exciting introduction to a report on this basketball game.

CHAPTER 2

DEVELOPING YOUR TOPIC

Showing off isn't always the best behavior. But writing a report is your chance to show off in the best possible way. Your report can offer readers information they don't already have. The more you give, the better.

Body paragraphs are the place for this knowledge. In this section of your report, you'll include all the details to develop your topic and explain it to readers. Give concrete details to support your writing. For example, when describing this photo you could write, "The lily pads are green."

The details you discover in your research might come from studies, articles, or real people who lived through events you need to describe. They are experts on your subject, and their stories can be powerful. It's up to you how to present them. You can paraphrase what they have to say. Or you can even quote them directly in your report.

WRITING PROMPT: INCLUDING QUOTES

Write one page of dialogue between two characters who are planning a party. Give the characters contrasting moods, such as happy and sad. After you finish, circle the lines of dialogue that you think are most important to the scene. These might be lines that are funny or that move the action along. Whichever lines you choose, they should be central to the conversation.

Most of a written report focuses on facts. It's important to gather facts from reliable sources, such as books, articles, and experts. You should also check the facts to be sure they're correct. If you find information from an article, for example, you could check it with an expert.

In the research process, you might also find out how other people feel about these facts. You might realize you have feelings about the facts too. Do your opinions, or feelings, belong in your report?

Reports aren't opinion pieces. But sometimes learning opinions about facts helps readers understand the facts better. It's important to recognize the difference between facts and opinions. A fact might be, "Tomatoes are red." An opinion might be, "I think tomatoes are delicious." Knowing the difference between facts and opinions can help you make well-informed decisions about whether or not opinions belong in your report.

WRITING PROMPT: FACTS VS. OPINIONS

Write two lists. In one, list facts you can gather from this photo. Include details you can see, such as objects and colors. In the other, list opinions you have about the photo. Describe how you feel about what you see.

Some topics have a ton of information available. You might start researching and find facts, opinions, descriptive details, quotes, images, and more. Everything seems important, and you may want to include it all. That's fine in a first draft. Your job as a writer will be easier in the long run if you have too much material rather than too little. Later in the process you can cut some information and refocus your report.

WRITING PROMPT: WRITE LONG

Set a timer for fifteen minutes. Use that time to write a piece about your favorite class, including facts and opinions. When you're done, read over your writing and write one sentence that tells the main idea of the story.

2 + 4 = 6
+ 8 =
+ 15 =

CHAPTER 3

DELIVERING YOUR INFORMATION

In a report, you need to give readers all the information they need to understand your topic. Certain details might be obvious to you. After all, you've researched your subject. You have all the answers. But this information might be completely unknown to readers when they pick up your piece. Consider your readers as you write. Try to imagine all the questions they might have about your topic.

Reports have plenty of text, but they can also include visuals, such as photos, illustrations, graphs, and charts. Visuals help when you want to show the information you're describing. Instead of imagining things, readers can see exactly what you mean.

WRITING PROMPT: ALL THE FACTS

Imagine you are a newspaper journalist assigned to interview a firefighter who recently put out a large fire. What will you ask? Create a list of questions that start with *Who*, *What*, *Where*, *Why*, *When*, and *How*.

Is your report about a specific subject? Of course it is! That means there might be specific vocabulary words related to the topic. But readers might need help understanding them. On a playground, some vocabulary words include *slide* and *swings*. Most readers will know these words.

Other vocabulary words might be less well-known. How can you help the reader understand them? Maybe after using a new vocabulary word, you could add a sentence explaining what the word means. Using the playground example, you might write, "Playgrounds have swings. These are rounded seats attached to a tall base by ropes or chains." Or you might choose to avoid new vocabulary words and use simpler language in your report that readers will be more likely to understand.

WRITING PROMPT: SIMPLIFYING

Write a short piece about this underwater creature. Don't worry about calling it by its correct name or using scientific terms to describe how it looks. Just use the words you know to describe what you see.

Writing a report starts with research. But as you're writing, you may find you need more information to fully explain your topic to readers. The good news is that research doesn't have to stop just because you've started your draft.

Doing extra research may take more time, but it doesn't have to feel like work. Think of yourself as a detective solving the "case" of the missing information in your report. Where will you look? Will you go to the library? Will you ask an expert in your subject for help?

WRITING PROMPT: DIGGING DEEPER

Imagine you have to explain how a car engine works. How can you find out? Who can you ask about it? What details do you need to know?

CHAPTER 4

PUTTING IT ALL TOGETHER

As you write, think about how to link your ideas together. Conjunctions are words such as *and* or *but* that connect phrases. They can help you connect your ideas. They're also useful for writing a strong conclusion. In your conclusion paragraph, you'll wrap up and restate important information from your report.

Once your draft is finished, you can share it with readers to get their feedback. Do they have questions after reading? Questions can help you see where you might need to add more information.

WRITING PROMPT: USING CONJUNCTIONS

Write a report about a person riding a horse for the first time. Include the conjunctions *because*, *however*, *but*, and *also*.

Your own opinion of your report is important too. Reread your draft and evaluate it yourself. Does it make sense to you? Do you think it's strong enough? You might decide it only needs small changes, such as rewriting a few sentences. Or you may decide your report needs a major rewrite. For example, you could discover a better way to organize and present your ideas.

After editing to catch spelling errors or grammatical mistakes, your work is done. Hopefully your report will earn a great grade. Maybe you'll even publish it online, in your school newspaper, or in a children's magazine!

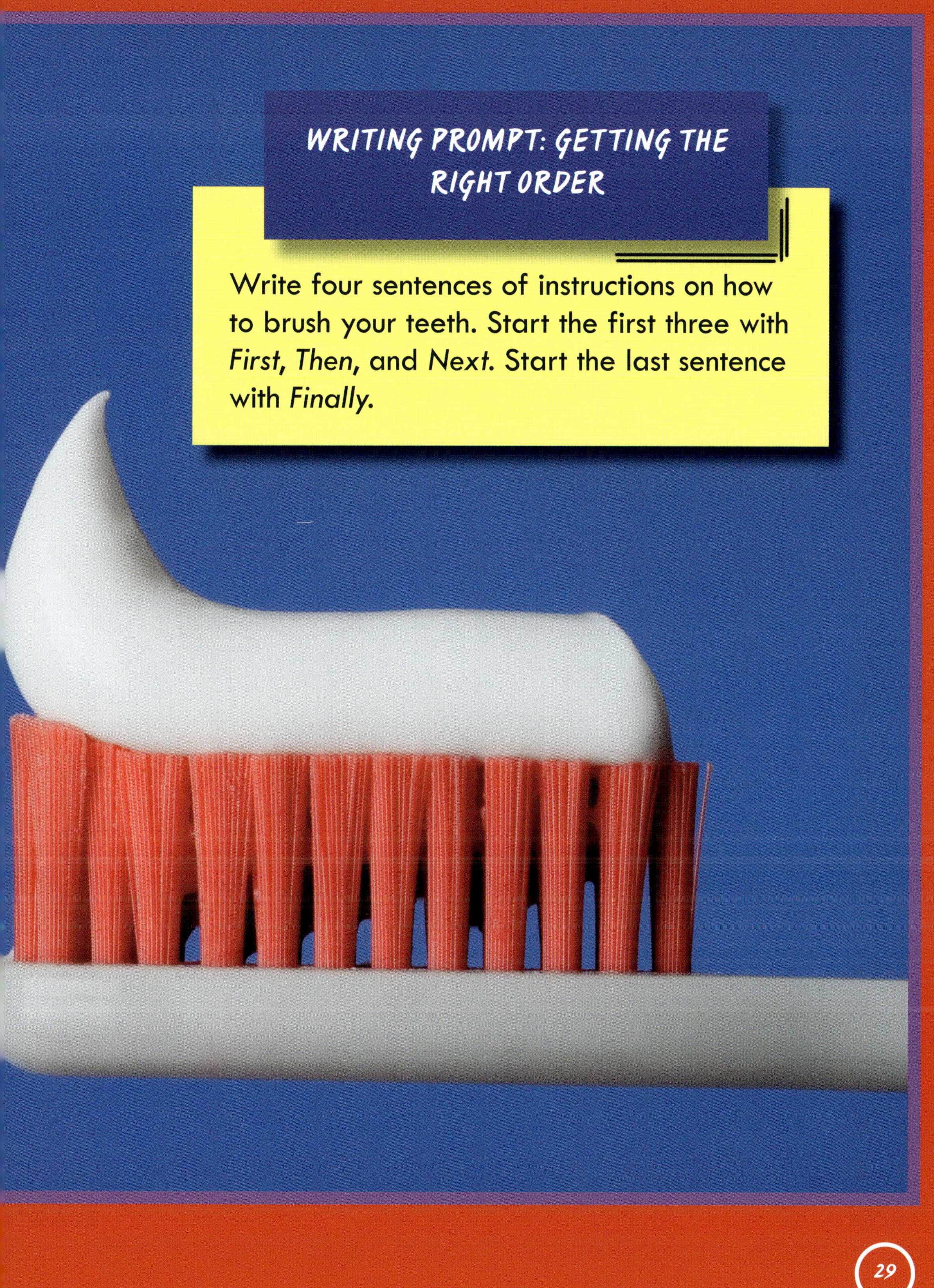

WRITING PROMPT: GETTING THE RIGHT ORDER

Write four sentences of instructions on how to brush your teeth. Start the first three with *First*, *Then*, and *Next*. Start the last sentence with *Finally*.

GLOSSARY

alliteration: using the same first letters in a series of words

dialogue: a conversation between different people in a written piece

draft: a written version of a piece of writing

edit: to correct or improve a piece of writing

evaluate: to carefully review, study, or judge something, such as a piece of writing

expert: a person who has education, experience, or knowledge on a specific subject

feedback: opinions, corrections, or comments given to a writer by a reader

paraphrase: to express the meaning of what someone said using different words than they did

publish: to make available to the public, such as in a newspaper or magazine

quote: to repeat something someone else said using their exact words and giving that person credit

revise: to change or rewrite a piece of writing to improve it

LEARN MORE

Britannica Kids: Journalist
https://kids.britannica.com/kids/article/journalist/624464

Holleran, Leslie. *Writing Fiction*. Lerner Publications, 2026.

Kiddle: Report Facts for Kids
https://kids.kiddle.co/Report

National Geographic Kids: How to Research Like a Pro
https://kids.nationalgeographic.com/homework-help/article/how-to-research-like-a-pro

Neely, Jenna. *Writing Skills*. Cherry Lake, 2024.

Rebman, Nick. *Writing a Report*. Focus Readers, 2024.

Schwartz, Heather E. *Writing an Opinion Piece*. Lerner Publications, 2026.

Study.com: Difference Between Fact & Opinion
https://study.com/academy/lesson/video/difference-between-fact-opinion-lesson-for-kids.html

INDEX

body paragraph, 7, 10, 13

conclusion, 7, 26
conjunction, 26–27

detail, 7, 13–14, 17–18, 20, 24
draft, 5, 7–8, 18, 24, 27–28

edit, 5, 28

fact, 4, 10, 16–18
feedback, 5, 27

introduction, 7–8, 10

opinion, 16–18, 28

publish, 5, 28

quote, 14, 18

research, 6, 14, 16, 18, 20, 24

title, 8
topic, 4–7, 10, 13, 18, 20, 22, 24

visual, 21

PHOTO ACKNOWLEDGMENTS

Image credits: Krakenimages.com/Shutterstock, p. 4; Klaus Vedfelt/Getty Images, p. 6; Alistair Berg/Getty Images, p. 7; hirohito takada/Getty Images, p. 9; Inti St Clair/Getty Images, p. 11; Tom Werner/Getty Images, p. 12; Lecristina/Getty Images, p. 13; Fiordaliso/Getty Images, p. 15; Peter Zvonar/Getty Images, p. 17; FG Trade/Getty Images, p. 19; Jose Luis Pelaez Inc/Getty Images, p. 20; Davin G Photography/Getty Images, p. 21; d3_plus D.Naruse @ Japan/Getty Images, p. 23; thirty_three/Getty Images, p. 25; RobinOlimb/Getty Images, p. 26; Lucas Ninno/Getty Images, p. 27; Glowimages/Getty Images, p. 29. Design elements: Olex Runda/Shutterstock; Claudio Divizia/Shutterstock.

Cover: damircudic/Getty Images.